Everything about Black Holes Astronomy Books Grade 6

Astronomy & Space Science

BABY PROFESSOR

EDUCATION KIDS

Speedy Publishing LLC
40 E. Main St. #1156
Newark, DE 19711
www.speedypublishing.com

How big are black holes? And how do astronomers study them in space? Many questions arise just from thinking about black holes.

Some people don't believe that black holes exist, while others do. Let's learn about the mystery of black holes.

Formation of Black Holes

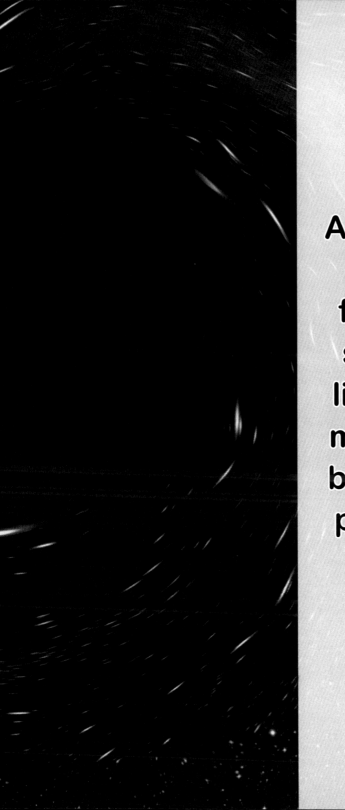

A black hole is a place in space where the force of gravity is so strong that not even light can escape. The most common type of black hole is when it's produced from a star at the end of its life.

The majority of stars have a balance of gravity and pressure which makes a star stable. But when a star runs out of nuclear fuel, the pressure of the star is pressed down making the star smaller and smaller until it becomes a black hole.

When a very large and heavy star runs out of fuel it explodes into a supernova. But when a small star's fuel is exhausted, the repulsive force of electrons inside the star produces enough pressure to stop a gravitational collapse. Its life ends peacefully and this is known as white dwarf.

Types of Black Holes

There are three types of black holes: primordial, stellar, and supermassive. The type of black holes depends on their sizes.

Primordial black holes are the smallest type and can be as small as an atom but with a mountain's mass.

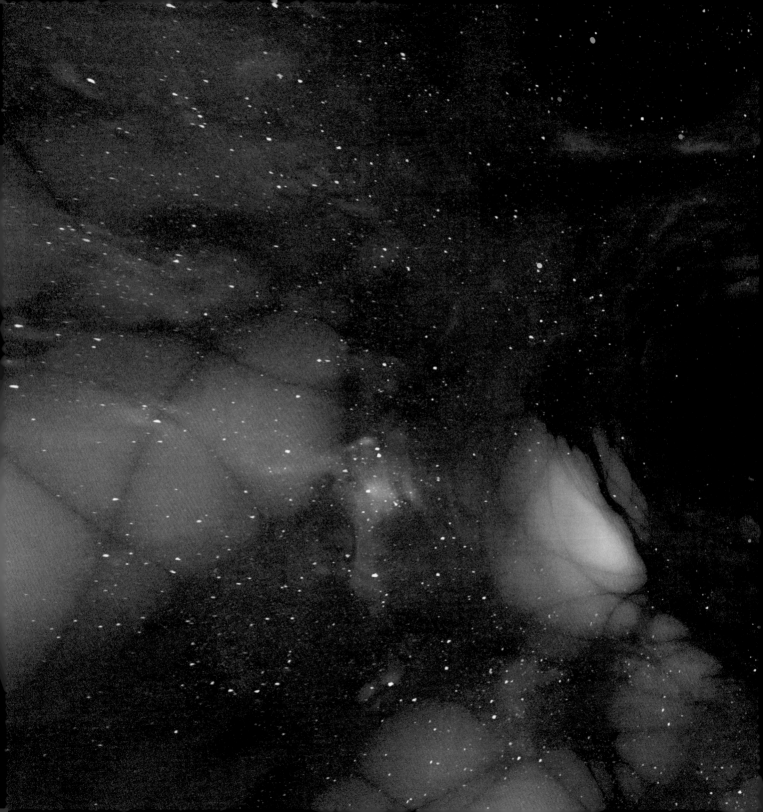

Stellars are the most common type of black holes, and reaches up to 20 times bigger and heavier than the Sun. There are dozens of stellar type black holes within the Milky Way.

Supermassive black holes are more than 1 million times bigger and heavier than the Sun. The formation of this type of black hole is still being examined.

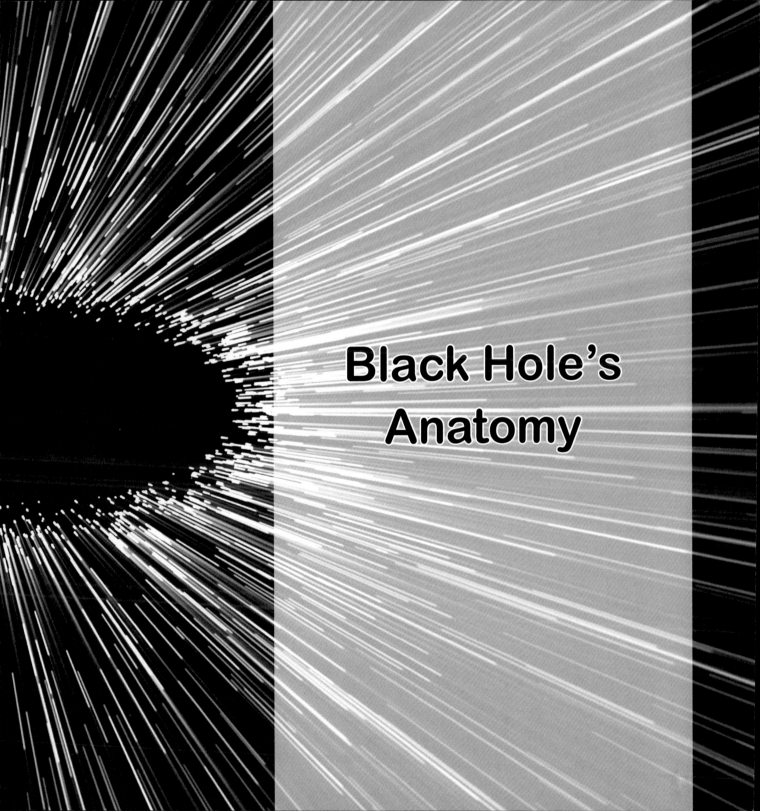

Black Hole's Anatomy

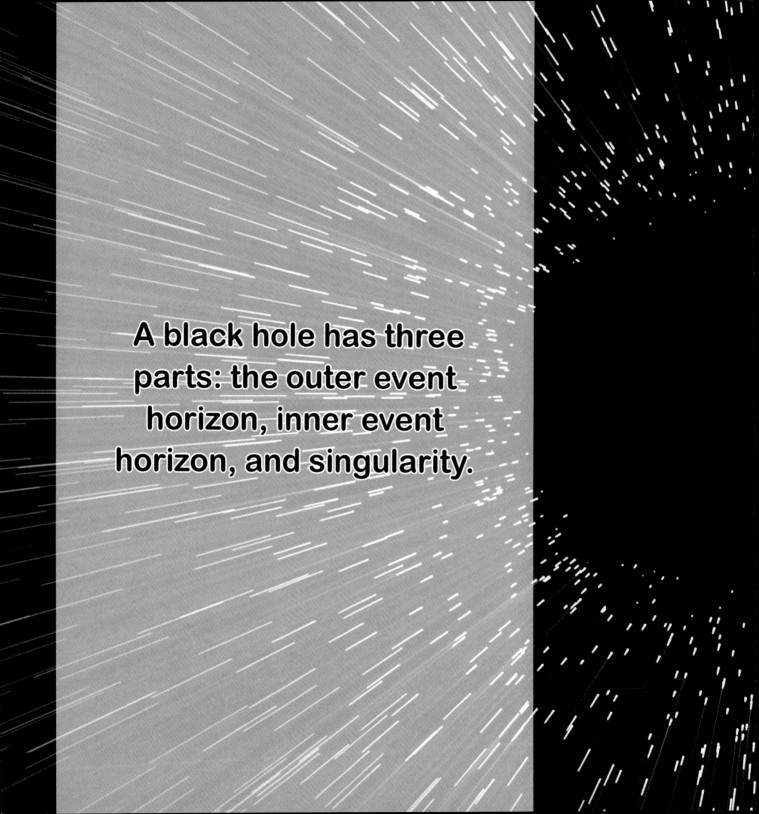

A black hole has three parts: the outer event horizon, inner event horizon, and singularity.

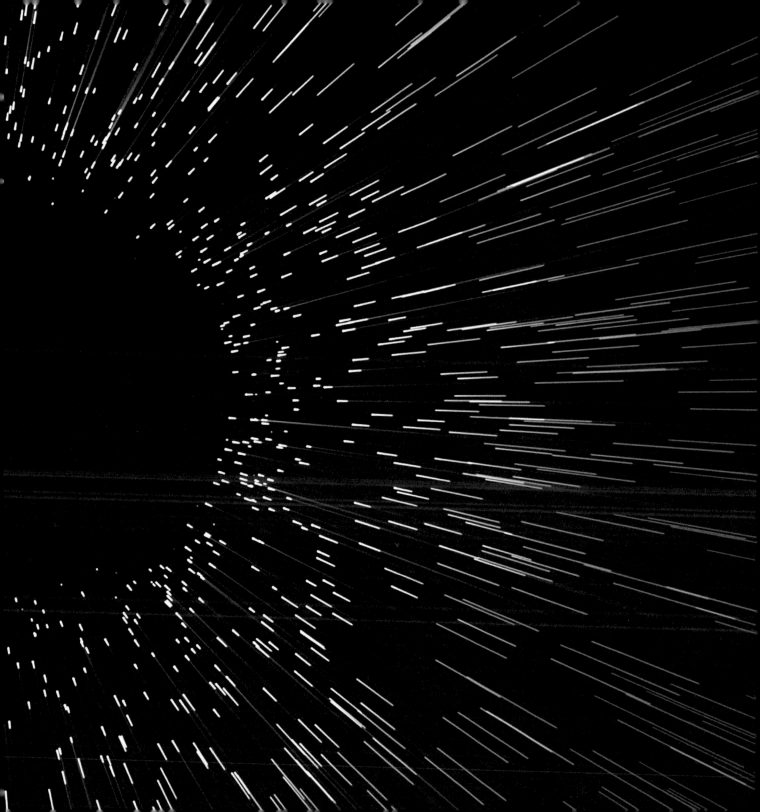

The Outer Event Horizon is the outside layer of a black hole. The gravity of the black hole in this layer is not that strong, so some objects can still escape from its gravity.

The black hole's middle layer is known as the inner event horizon. Its gravity is much stronger. Once it captures an object it doesn't let go of it again.

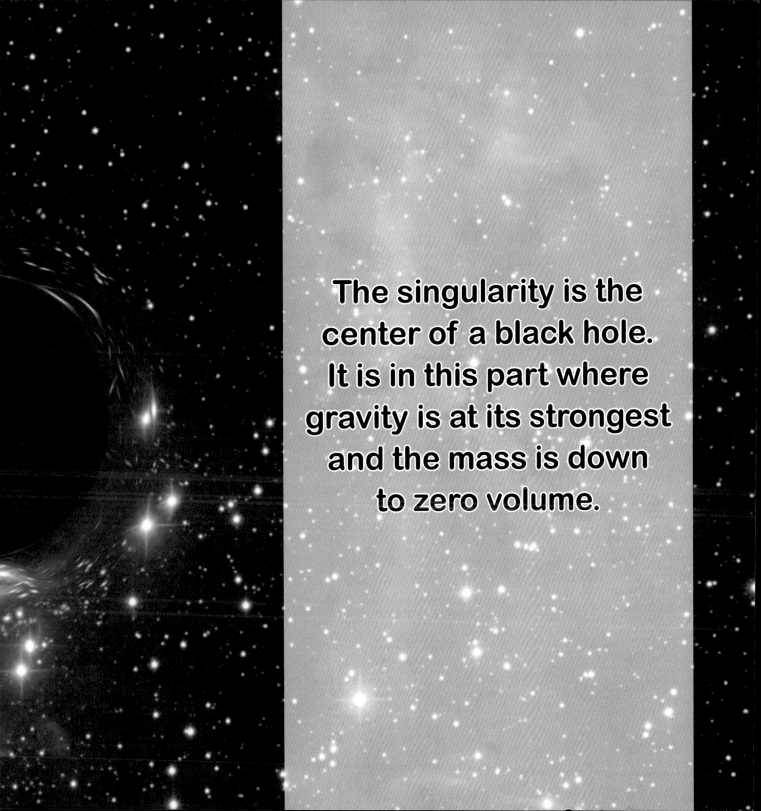

The singularity is the center of a black hole. It is in this part where gravity is at its strongest and the mass is down to zero volume.

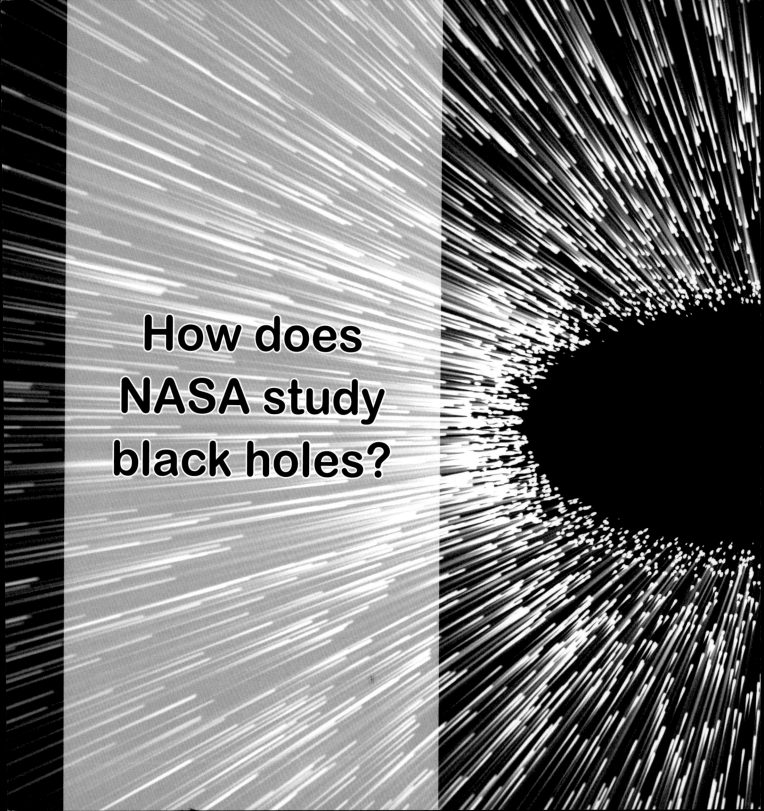

How does
NASA study
black holes?

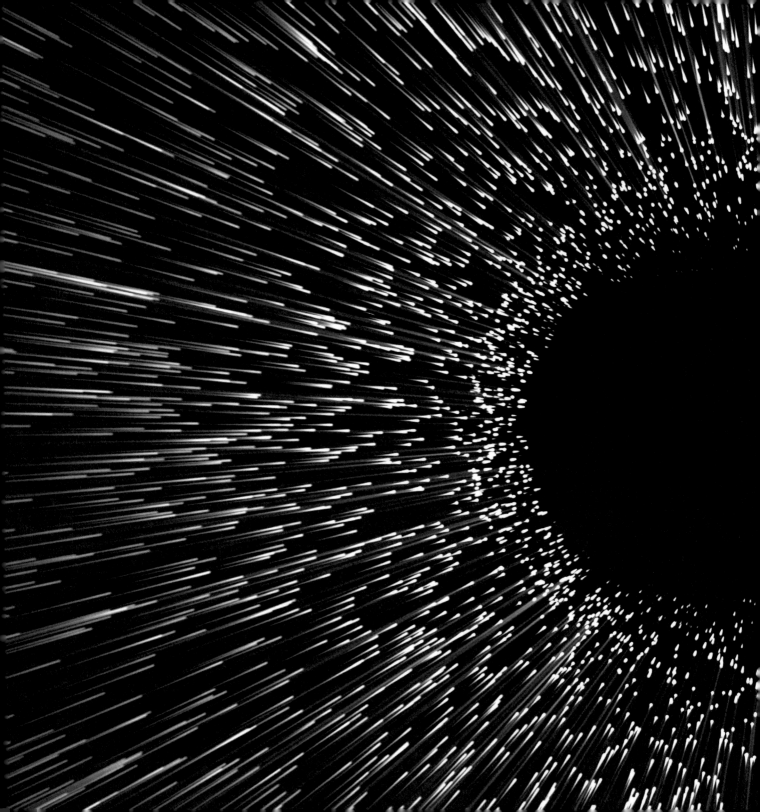

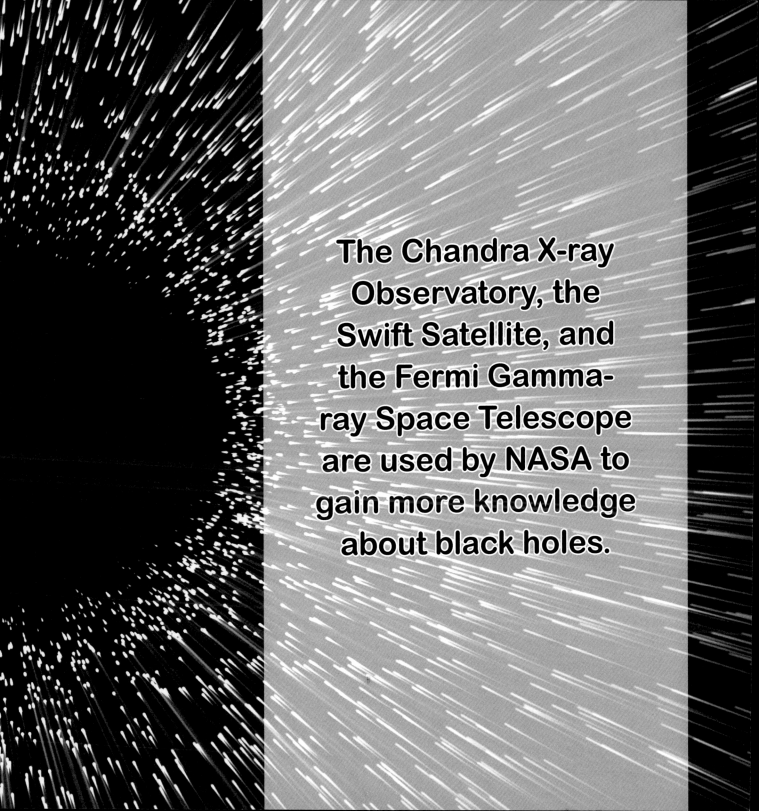

The Chandra X-ray Observatory, the Swift Satellite, and the Fermi Gamma-ray Space Telescope are used by NASA to gain more knowledge about black holes.

Fermi was launched
in 2008 to observe
gamma rays in space,
find supermassive black
holes and observe other
phenomena in space.

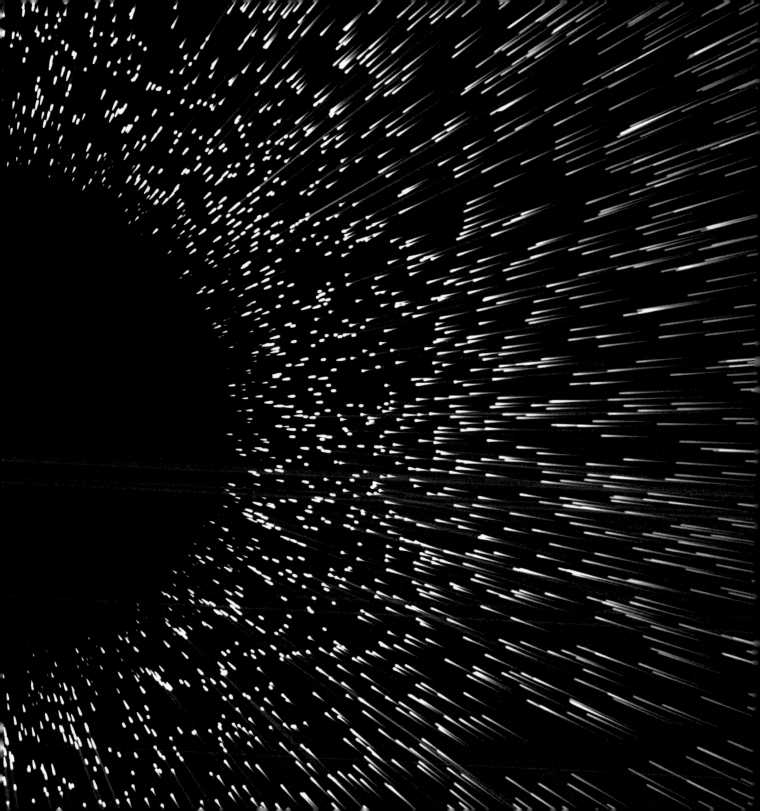

Observing black holes with telescopes that can discover x-rays, lights or electromagnetic radiation is not possible.

The presence of black holes in space can be detected by observing its gravity's effect on the matter that surrounds it like the stars and gases.

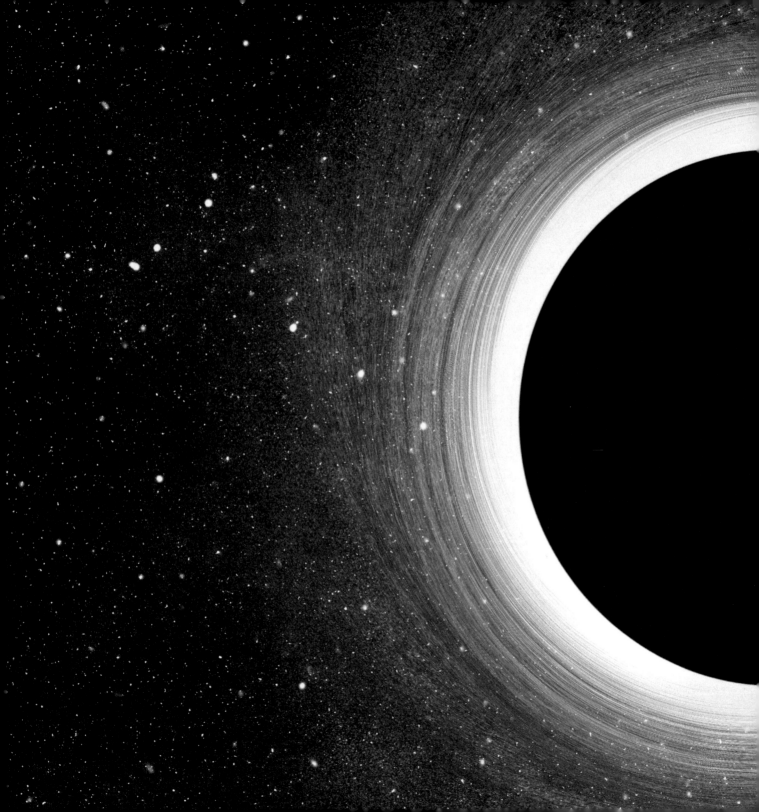

When a star and a
black hole are closely
orbiting together they
produce high-energy
light, and this light can
be viewed by specialized
scientific instruments.

Could a black hole destroy a planet?

Just like other celestial objects in space, black holes are also affected by the law of gravity. It can't just destroy or swallow a planet as it likes.

The Earth can't be affected by black holes unless they are already very close, inside our solar system.

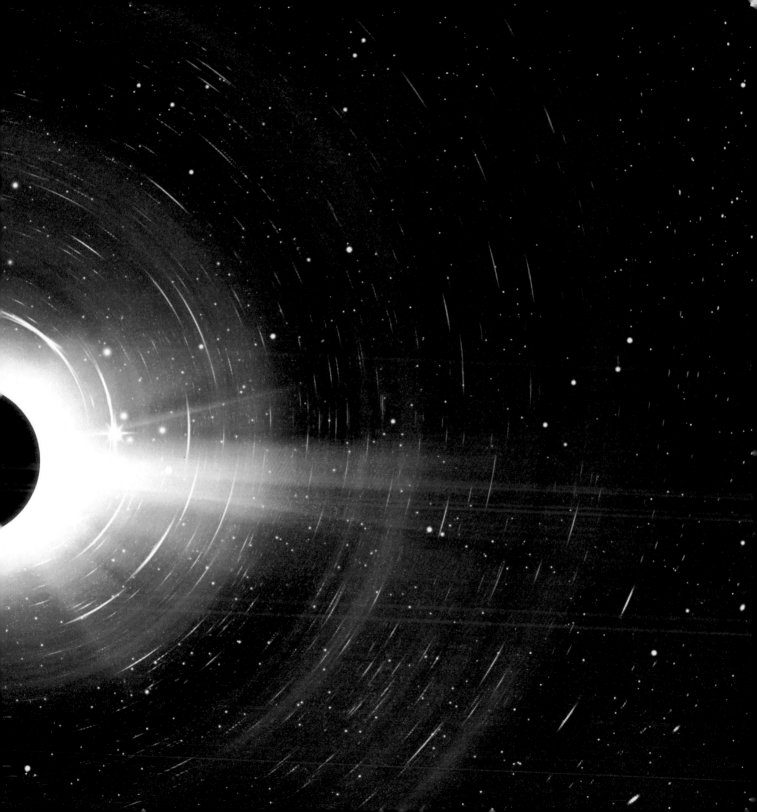

Even if a black hole
replaces a sun, if it
has the same mass as
the sun, it still won't
affect any planet
in the universe.

Black holes with the same gravity of the sun, replacing the sun, would let the planets continue in their orbits. However, there would be no sunlight or warmth for the planets to use.

The sun can't collapse into a black hole because it doesn't have enough mass. When the time comes that the sun's life comes to an end, it will only turn into a red giant start.

And when it runs out of nuclear fuel, the outside layer of the sun will be thrown off, turning into a bright ring of gas known as a planetary nebula. Then our sun would become a white dwarf star.

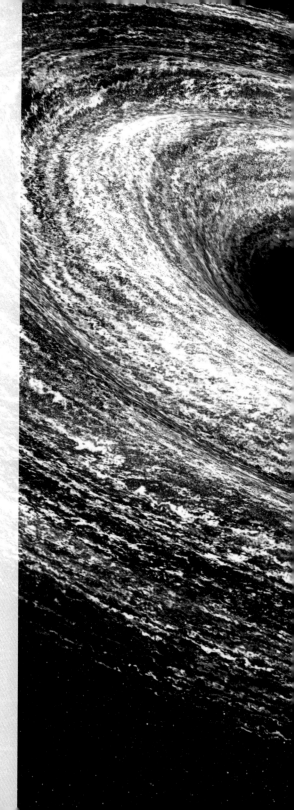

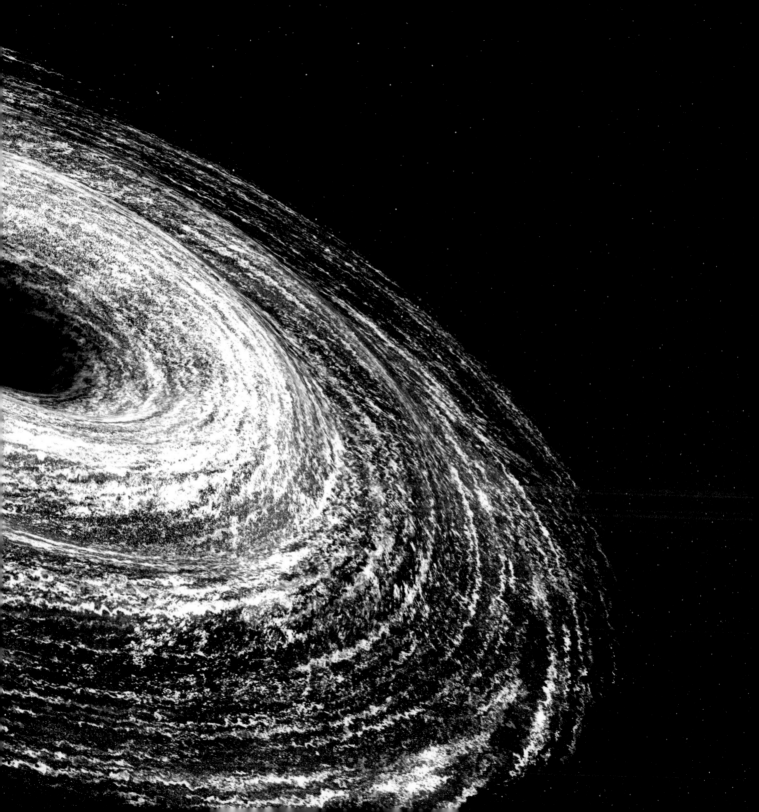

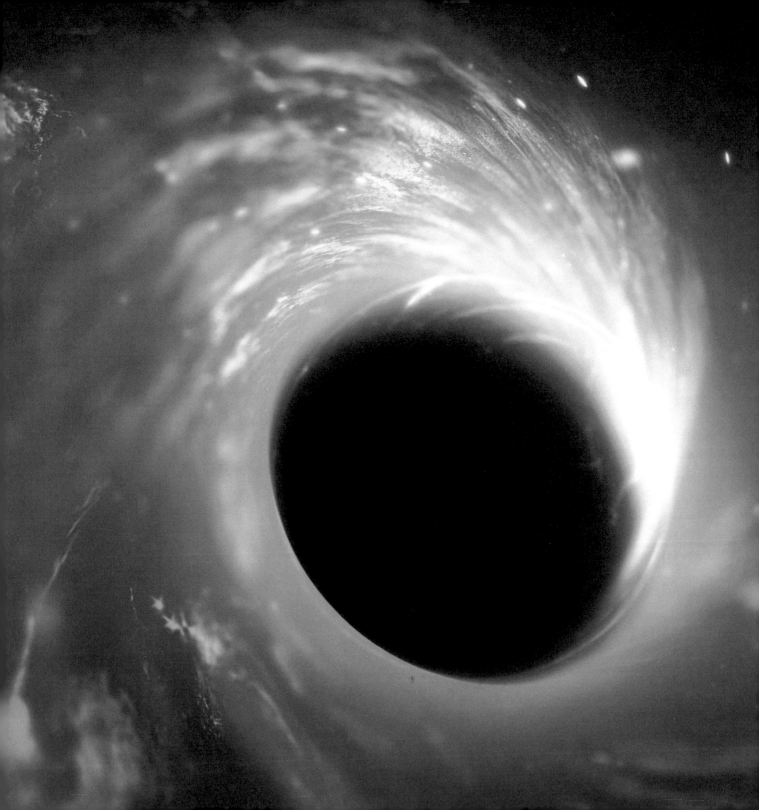

Whether black holes exist or not, knowing the observations of our scientists about this feature of space in the universe is an advantage for us. This is the wonder of science!

There is more to
know about the black
holes. Research more
and have fun!

Visit

BABY PROFESSOR
EDUCATION KIDS

www.BabyProfessorBooks.com

to download Free Baby Professor eBooks
and view our catalog of new and exciting
Children's Books

Made in the USA
San Bernardino, CA
09 October 2018